MANATEES

NATIONAL GEOGRAPHIC
Little
kids™

OCEAN COUNTING

By Janet Lawler
Photographs by Brian Skerry

NATIONAL
GEOGRAPHIC

WASHINGTON, D.C.

4

Explore our beautiful blue ocean while learning how to count. Visit colorful coral reefs, warm and sunny seas, sparkling ice packs, and other special spots where marine animals live and play. And on your way, discover new ocean friends on a worldwide counting adventure.

Are you ready? Let's dive in!

BLACK SEA URCHIN IN CORAL REEF

1 green sea turtle

One green sea turtle swims and skims along the ocean floor. It chomps on a meal of sea grass. See what looks like a puff of smoke? It is the sandy sea bottom stirred up by the turtle's feeding.

Did you know?
Green sea turtles often swim hundreds of miles (km) to lay eggs on the same beach where they were born.

2 harp seals

Two harp seals nuzzle, nose to nose, in the icy Arctic. Guess which is the baby. Did you choose the soft, fuzzy, yellow one? Mother seal stays close to feed her new pup.

Did you know?

A harp seal mother finds her pup in a huge crowd of seals by sniffing for its scent.

3

star-eye parrotfish

Three star-eye parrotfish show colors as bright as a tropical bird. What else about this fish reminds you of a parrot? The strong teeth of these fish are tightly packed into a parrotlike beak.

Did you know?

Many parrotfish blanket themselves with gooey mucus before sleeping at night.

4 reef squid

Four reef squid explore shallow waters. What color are they now? Faster than a blink they can change colors or patterns. They do this to signal each other, blend in, find mates, or warn enemies.

Did you know?

A squid's many arms are attached in a circle around its mouth.

5
pink sea star arms

Five arms on this pink sea star bend and flex.
Tube-like suckers underneath these arms hold
the sea star in place. What else do the suckers
do? They grab food and help the sea star move.

Did you know?
If an arm breaks off, a sea star can grow another one.

15

6 Adélie penguins

Six Adélie penguins waddle over ice toward open water. Which penguin looks ready to dive in? Maybe it is just picking up a stone to line its nest.

Did you know?
Young Adélies begin to swim on their own at about nine weeks old.

7 glass eye fish

Seven glass eye fish dart and dip around coral. Their shiny red scales dazzle like flashes of fire. Can you also count seven big black eyes?

Did you know?

The young of this kind of glass eye fish are spotted brown and red.

8 sea otters

Eight sea otters doze in a cozy group, floating on their backs. How do they stay dry and warm? Their thick, slick fur acts like a raincoat and traps air to keep out the cold.

21

9 hammerhead sharks

Nine hammerhead sharks swim together. The sun shines down on them through clear sky and water. How do you think this shark got its name? Its head is shaped like a hammer.

Did you know?

Hammerhead sharks can tan from the sun.

10 Bermuda sea chub

Ten Bermuda sea chub glide, tails waving side to side, above a colorful reef. Where are they going? Maybe they will visit nearby sea plants to nibble a snack.

Did you know?

Sea chub swim in schools. A school is a large number of one kind of fish swimming together.

Now that you have finished your counting adventure, let's count our animal friends again from one to ten!

1 green sea turtle

2 harp seals

3 star-eye parrotfish

4 reef squid

5 pink sea stars

6 Adélie penguins

7 glass eye fish

8 sea otters

9 hammerhead sharks

10 Bermuda sea chub

Now let's count down from ten to one!

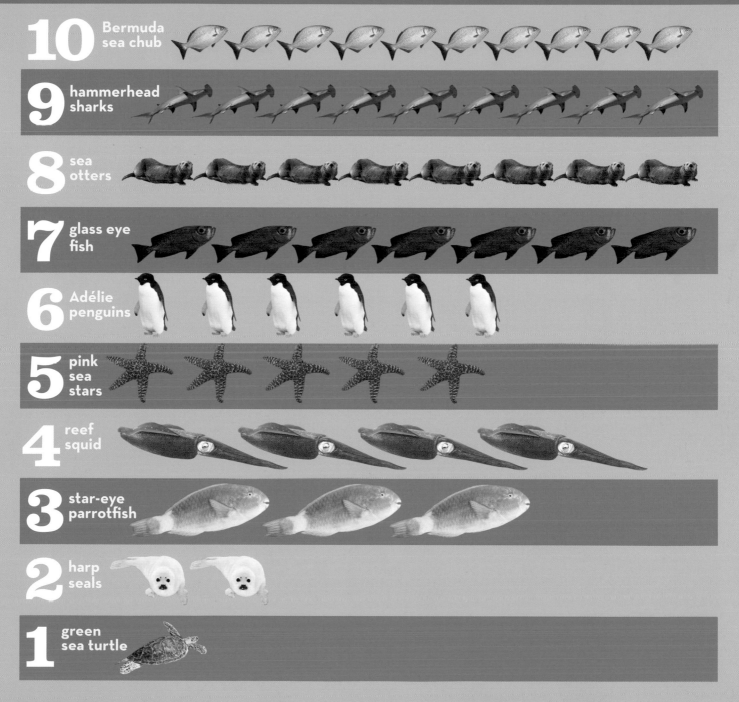

10 Bermuda sea chub

9 hammerhead sharks

8 sea otters

7 glass eye fish

6 Adélie penguins

5 pink sea stars

4 reef squid

3 star-eye parrotfish

2 harp seals

1 green sea turtle

ANIMAL FACTS

1 GREEN SEA TURTLE

HOME: warm and tropical coastal waters, reefs, bays, and inlets
SIZE: about the size of a large truck tire
FOOD: sea plants, squids, crabs, and other small sea dwellers; adults eat mostly sea grasses
PREDATORS: for adults: large sharks; for hatchlings: crabs, shore birds, and small meat-eaters like foxes, dogs, and cats
BABIES: females lay about 75–200 eggs at a time, burying them on a beach

2 HARP SEALS

HOME: North Atlantic and Arctic Oceans
SIZE: weighs about as much as two adult humans
FOOD: small fish, including cod, herring, and capelin; shrimp and other crustaceans
PREDATORS: polar bears, killer whales, and sharks
BABIES: one, born on pack ice

3 STAR-EYE PARROTFISH

HOME: warm and tropical rocky and coral reefs
SIZE: about as long as a cat
FOOD: seaweed and algae
PREDATORS: eels, sharks, larger fish, and octopuses
BABIES: females lay eggs

4 CARIBBEAN REEF SQUID

HOME: the Caribbean Sea
SIZE: about as long as a pencil
FOOD: small fish, other squid, snails, slugs, and shrimp and other crustaceans
PREDATORS: large fish, including yellowfin grouper and snapper; eels
BABIES: females lay 7-8 eggs in a capsule deposited on the sea bottom, usually on dirt, rocks, sand, or gravel

5 PINK SEA STAR

HOME: found in shallow to deep waters in all oceans
SIZE: can grow to about the size of a large pizza
FOOD: clams, sand dollars, snails, mussels, barnacles, and tube worms
PREDATORS: seagulls
BABIES: females and males release gametes that join in the water

6

ADÉLIE PENGUINS

HOME: Antarctica
SIZE: weighs about as much as a very large watermelon
FOOD: tiny shrimplike krill, fish, and squid
PREDATORS: at sea: leopard seals and killer whales; on land: giant petrels and skuas
BABIES: one (sometimes two), hatched in a rock-lined nest

7

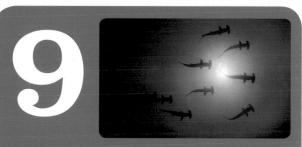

GLASS EYE FISH

HOME: coral reefs worldwide
SIZE: about as long as a man's foot
FOOD: small fish, plankton, and other invertebrates
PREDATORS: bony fish and sea birds
BABIES: females scatter many eggs in the water

8

SEA OTTERS

HOME: shallow coastal waters of the Pacific Ocean off of North America and Asia
SIZE: about the size of a large dog
FOOD: clams, mussels, urchins, crabs, squid, octopuses, snails, and fish
PREDATORS: for adults: killer whales, sharks, and sea lions; for pups: bald eagles
BABIES: one, born in water

9

HAMMERHEAD SHARKS

HOME: warm and tropical seas, bays, and lagoons
SIZE: about as long as a small car
FOOD: many bony fishes, squid, octopuses, other sharks, rays, crabs, and lobsters
PREDATORS: larger sharks
BABIES: about 12–36, born live in the ocean

10

BERMUDA SEA CHUB

HOME: shallow waters of the Atlantic Ocean, mostly off Florida, USA, Caribbean islands, and the Gulf of Mexico; some in the Mediterranean Sea
SIZE: about the length of a child's baseball bat
FOOD: mostly sea plants and algae
PREDATORS: sharks, barracuda, and other large fish
BABIES: females lay many eggs in the water

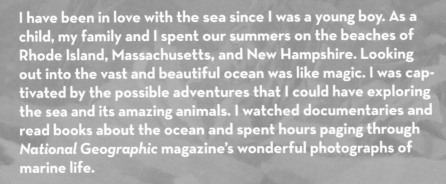

I have been in love with the sea since I was a young boy. As a child, my family and I spent our summers on the beaches of Rhode Island, Massachusetts, and New Hampshire. Looking out into the vast and beautiful ocean was like magic. I was captivated by the possible adventures that I could have exploring the sea and its amazing animals. I watched documentaries and read books about the ocean and spent hours paging through *National Geographic* magazine's wonderful photographs of marine life.

As a grown-up, I have had the chance to follow my dreams of exploration as an underwater photojournalist, taking pictures all over the world. The pictures in this book were taken on some of my adventures. The map on the next page will show you where I was when I took each photo. The map key will help you identify each animal and find its location. As you take your own adventure through this book, I hope you will be inspired, as I was, to learn more about the ocean and the incredible creatures that call it home.

—Brian Skerry

Where the Pictures Were Taken

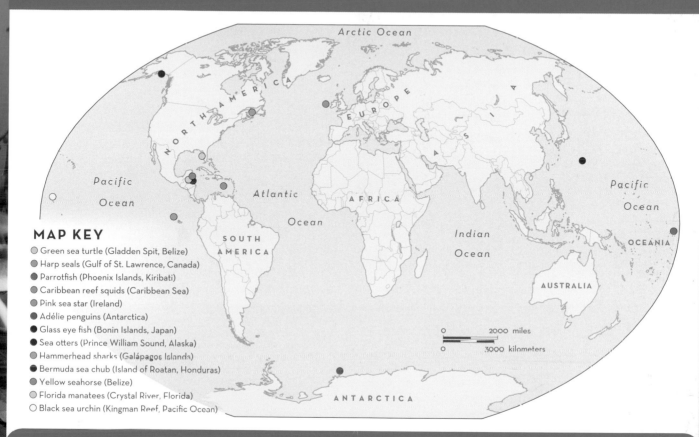

MAP KEY
- Green sea turtle (Gladden Spit, Belize)
- Harp seals (Gulf of St. Lawrence, Canada)
- Parrotfish (Phoenix Islands, Kiribati)
- Caribbean reef squids (Caribbean Sea)
- Pink sea star (Ireland)
- Adélie penguins (Antarctica)
- Glass eye fish (Bonin Islands, Japan)
- Sea otters (Prince William Sound, Alaska)
- Hammerhead sharks (Galápagos Islands)
- Bermuda sea chub (Island of Roatan, Honduras)
- Yellow seahorse (Belize)
- Florida manatees (Crystal River, Florida)
- Black sea urchin (Kingman Reef, Pacific Ocean)

Let's use this map to have some counting fun!

➡ **Count the ocean names. How many are there?**

➡ **Count each named land area (continent). How many are there?**

   Are there more oceans or more continents?

➡ **Count every spot where a picture was taken. How many are there?**

GLOSSARY

ALGAE: simple, plantlike ocean organisms

CAPELIN: a small fish found in the Atlantic and Arctic Oceans

CRUSTACEANS: animals, such as crabs, that have a hard outer covering

GAMETE: a female or male basic cell that can grow into a creature

GIANT PETREL: a large sea bird with a wingspan as wide as an adult human's outstretched arms

INVERTEBRATES: animals that do not have backbones

LAGOON: an area of shallow water separated from the ocean by a reef or islands

MUCUS: a jelly-like slime that some fish produce to coat and protect themselves

PREDATORS: animals that kill and eat other animals

SKUA: a sea bird about the size of a large seagull

TROPICAL: in a part of the world where it is very hot year-round

MORE INFORMATION

For more information about ocean animals, check out these books and websites.

BOOKS

Davies, Nicola. *Science Kids: Oceans and Seas.* New York, NY: Kingfisher, 2007.

Earle, Sylvia A. *Coral Reefs.* Washington, DC: National Geographic, 2009.

Halfmann, Janet. *Star of the Sea: A Day in the Life of a Starfish.* New York, NY: Henry Holt & Company, 2011.

Momatiuk, Yva and Eastcott, John. *Face to Face with Penguins.* Washington, DC: National Geographic, 2009.

Rizzo, Johnna and Sylvia Earle. *Oceans.* Washington, DC: National Geographic, 2010.

Rustad, Martha E.H. *Parrotfish.* Minneapolis, MN: Bellweather Media, 2008.

Sayre, April Pulley. *Turtle, Turtle, Watch Out!* New York, NY: Orchard Books, 2000.

Skerry, Brian. *Face to Face with Manatees.* Washington, DC: National Geographic, 2010.

Stierle, Cynthia. *Ocean Life from A to Z.* Pleasantville, NY: Readers Digest Children's Books, 2007.

WEBSITES

National Geographic Kids: kids.nationalgeographic.com/kids/animals

National Geographic: animals.nationalgeographic.com/animals

National Geographic: ocean.nationalgeographic.com/ocean

National Aquarium: www.aqua.org

Earth's Kids: earthskids.com/ek_science-marine.htm

Monterey Bay Aquarium: montereybayaquarium.org

Shedd Aquarium: sheddaquarium.org

Answers to map questions: 1. There are 4 oceans. 2. There are 7 continents. There are more continents than oceans. 3. There are 13 picture locations.

National Geographic's net proceeds support vital exploration, conservation, research, and education programs.

**‹125›
YEARS**

Text copyright © 2013 Janet Lawler
Illustrations copyright © 2013 Brian Skerry
Compilation copyright © 2013 National Geographic Society.
Published by the National Geographic Society, Washington, D.C. 20036. All rights reserved. Reproduction in whole or in part without written permission of the publisher is strictly prohibited.

Photo Credits: All images are by Brian J. Skerry unless otherwise noted below:

20-21 and 29 (8), Michael Deyoung/National Geographic Stock; 22-23 and 29 (9), Norbert Probst/Newscom; 30 (inset), Mauricio Handler/National Geographic Stock

For more information, please call 1-800-NGS LINE (647-5463) or write to the following address:

National Geographic Society
1145 17th Street N.W.
Washington, D.C. 20036-4688 U.S.A.

Visit us online at www.nationalgeographic.com/books

Hardcover ISBN: 978-1-4263-1116-1

Library edition ISBN: 978-1-4263-1117-8

Printed in China
13/TS/1